Wondrous Women

COLORING BOOK

Marty Noble

Dover Publications, Inc.
Mineola, New York

These captivating images feature elegant women in ethereal and natural settings, with beautiful backgrounds of butterflies, birds, flowers, and leaves. The fashionable figures are pictured in an array of stunning dresses and hairdos, incorporating Art Nouveau influences as well as nature motifs and signature styles from a wide range of cultures. Specially designed for the experienced colorist, the illustrations in this book will enchant and inspire you while you experiment with color and different media. Each of the thirty-one plates has been perforated for removal to make displaying your work easy.

Bibliographical Note

Wondrous Women Coloring Book is a new work,
first published by Dover Publications, Inc., in 2019.

International Standard Book Number

ISBN-13: 978-0-486-82846-6
ISBN-10: 0-486-82846-8

Manufactured in the United States by LSC Communications
82846801   2019
www.doverpublications.com